Old Glory

Jeanne and Bradley Weaver

Contents

Introduction

In 1824, a ship captain named William Driver was about to leave on a long sea journey. Before he sailed, his mother gave him a beautiful American flag. Captain Driver looked at the flag flying in the wind and thought, "How glorious!" He named the flag "**Old Glory**."

"Old Glory" has become a favorite name for the flag of the United States of America. The flag we use today is different from Captain Driver's "Old Glory." The story of how our flag came to be is a glorious one!

The Creation of Our Flag

The United States of America began as 13 **colonies**, or settlements, ruled by Great Britain. The colonies flew the British flag. This flag was called the Union Jack.

In 1775, American **colonists** decided they wanted to be free from Great Britain. They formed an army led by General George Washington. He decided that the colonies needed a flag of their own. This new flag was called the Grand Union flag. It added red and white stripes to the British flag. The red and white stripes stood for the 13 colonies.

George Washington

Union Jack flag

Grand Union flag

The Continental Congress met in 1777
to decide on the new American flag.

In 1776, the colonists declared their **independence**,
or freedom, from Great Britain. They set up a new
government called the **Continental Congress**. On
June 14, 1777, the Congress decided it was important
for the new country to have a new flag.

The Congress decided that the new flag should
have 13 red and white stripes. It should also have
13 white stars on a blue background. The stripes
would represent the 13 original colonies. The stars
would show that they were united as a nation.

The Congress did not provide any other instructions for how to make the flag. They didn't say how long the stripes should be. They didn't say how the stars should be arranged or how many points each star should have. As a result, there were many different designs for the new flag.

Many different flags were designed with 13 stars and stripes.

The First Flag

No one is sure who made the first American flag. Many people believe it was Betsy Ross. General Washington and other leaders asked her to sew a flag. Betsy Ross was a sewing expert. She could fold cloth and make a five-point star with one cut.

As the story goes, Betsy Ross stayed up all night sewing the first flag. The new flag was beautiful! People have searched for Betsy Ross's flag since, but it has never been found.

Betsy Ross designed a flag with 13 stars placed in a circle.

Our Growing Country

Over the years the United States has grown from 13 states to 50 states. Each time a new state was added, a star was added to the flag. In 1959, Alaska and Hawaii became the last two states to join our nation.

The **canton** is the upper area of the flag next to the flagstaff.

The **field** is the background color of the flag.

The **flagstaff** is a post that holds the flag up high.

The **fly** is the part of the flag that is farthest from the flagstaff.

Robert Heft

With the news of Alaska and Hawaii becoming states, a high school student had an idea for a school project. Robert Heft's idea was to create the new American flag. He didn't know how to sew, but he did his best and made a flag with 13 stripes and 50 stars.

Robert Heft today

When Robert brought his new flag to class, his teacher gave him a B-minus. The teacher told Robert that he could get a better grade if he could get the United States Congress to accept his design. To the teacher's surprise, Congress chose Robert's design as the new American flag.

Honoring Our Flag

There are many ways that Americans honor the flag. We sing the **national anthem**, or song. We say the **Pledge of Allegiance**. We also have a **flag code** that tells us when and how to use the flag.

The National Anthem

In 1814, Francis Scott Key stood on a ship near a dangerous battle. He watched an American flag flying over Fort McHenry. The fight lasted all night. When the sun rose, Francis Scott Key was thrilled to see the flag still flying! The Americans had won. Francis Scott Key wrote a poem about the battle. His poem became our national anthem. Today, people sing the national anthem to honor our flag.

The national anthem is sung at many sports events.

Children have been saying the Pledge of Allegiance at school since 1892.

The Pledge of Allegiance

In 1892, Francis Bellamy helped plan a special Columbus Day celebration. He wrote these words for the event.

"I pledge allegiance to my flag and to the Republic for which it stands—one nation indivisible—with liberty and justice for all."

Bellamy's pledge was given to schools across the country. In October 1892, about 12 million children said the pledge aloud for the first time.

In 1923, the words "my flag" were changed to "the flag of the United States of America." The pledge was changed again in 1954 when the words "under God" were added. Millions of school children still say the Pledge of Allegiance every morning.

Respecting the Flag

When saying the Pledge of Allegiance or singing the national anthem, Americans should:

★ Take off their hats.

★ Stand facing the flag.

★ Place their right hand over their heart.

The Flag Code

In 1923, a group of people wrote the flag code. The code is a set of rules for how to respect our flag. The flag code tells us when to use the flag and how to display it correctly.

More than one person is needed to raise and lower a flag correctly.

Flag Code Rules

These rules show us how to treat our flag with respect.

★ Fly the flag from sunrise to sunset.

★ Raise the flag quickly and lower it slowly.

★ Never let the flag touch the ground.

★ When the flag is old and ruined, destroy it rather than throwing it in the trash.

★ Fold the flag correctly into a triangle so only its stars are showing.

People fly the flag outside their homes on Flag Day.

Flag Day

In 1949, President Harry S. Truman made June 14 an official holiday. Flag Day is a day set aside for all Americans to celebrate the flag. This date was chosen because it is the anniversary of the day in 1777 when the Continental Congress decided to use a flag with stars and stripes to represent our country.

Portraits of Our Flag

Americans show pride in their country by displaying the flag and carrying it to new places. The American flag has traveled the world. It has even been flown on the moon.

An astronaut puts the United States flag on the moon.

Thousands of people in Tucson, Arizona, created this human flag.

A boy shows off the flag he's made out of popcorn and hotdogs.

Americans show their pride by decorating things with stars and stripes.

People have painted this house to look like the flag.

A Symbol of Freedom

Worldwide, the American flag is a **symbol** of freedom. To Americans, the many freedoms they have are glorious, just like Captain Driver thought so many years ago. When you look at the flag flying in the wind, think about what your freedom means to you!

Glossary

colonist — a person who lives in a colony

colony — a settlement far away from the country that rules it

Continental Congress — the first group of leaders elected to make laws in the United States of America

flag code — a set of rules that tell how and when to use the flag

independence — freedom

national anthem — the official song of a country

Old Glory — a nickname for the flag of the United States of America

Pledge of Allegiance — an oath to one's flag and country

symbol — something that stands for something else

Index